Max and the Clouds

words by Nigel Croser
illustrated by Neil Curtis

Min and Mop were eating grass.
Max was looking at the sky.
He was looking at the clouds.
"I can see a bird," he said.

"I can see a bird, too," said Min.

"We can all see a bird," said Mop.

Then the wind blew and the clouds changed.

"I can see a rabbit," said Max.

"I can see a rabbit, too," said Min.

"We can all see a rabbit," said Mop.

Then the clouds changed again.

"I can see a horse," said Max.

"I can see a horse, too," said Min.

"We can all see a horse," said Mop.

Then the clouds changed again.

"I can see a cow," said Max.

"I can see a cow, too," said Min.

"We can all see a cow," said Mop.

Then the clouds changed again.

"I can see a goat," said Max.
"I can see a goat, too," said Min.
"We can all see a goat," said Mop.
Then the clouds changed again.
"Hmm! I can see some sheep,"
said a fox.

"I can see a fox!" said Min.

"I can see a fox, too!" said Mop.

"I can't see a fox," said Max,

"but I can see a big lion."

"A lion?" said the fox.

"I'm going before the lion sees me!"